MW01710006

UNDERSTAND HINDI IN 20 DAYS

COMPILED BY SATASH SINGH

WWW.CARIBBEANTRAKKER.COM

This book is printed and published by Caribbean Trakker Inc.

Preface

Welcome to Understand Hindi in 20 days! To begin I would like to say that like you I also wanted to grasp a different language and for many years, I have tried to write the Hindi language. Many us believe that if we can write a specific language we can also read, speak and understand it. But this is far from the truth.

The four methods of writing, reading, speaking and understanding a language is what is needed to really say you know a language. All the senses help with this development of language just like a child. For example, to speak to someone you must be able to think, and to understand what someone is saying, you must comprehend. But just because you can read a language does not mean that you can write it, and the same way is for understanding a language it does not mean that you can speak it. Over the past few years I have tried to learn other languages like French and Spanish. I learned very fast to read them long before I could write them. For the matter of fact, I could read these languages fairly well before I could speak them.

Hindi is a challenging language to people who speak the English language as a first languauge, because of the construction of the Hindi sentences. The verb is in the end of Hindi sentence while in the English language it is in the middle of the sentence. This causes understanding the Hindi language to be confusing. For example, "nazdeek telefon kahan hai?" when translated is exactly to English is "near telephone where is?" I English it is 'Where is the nearest Telephone'.

As a pupil of the Hindi language I even tried taking Hindi classes to learn the language. After a while, I figured that I should research the language using all avenues open to me, including the web. I wanted to understand the Hindi songs that I listen to all the time, but never quite understood it.

This book is a direct compilation of my research. Let me say this, I do not profess to knowing the Hindi language, and sometimes I even worry that I even know the English language. I also do not make any representation that I can write, read, or speak Hindi; as I am still a learner of all these faculties.

I do hope that this book is of help to you if you are learning Hindi, as it is a beautiful language as a difficult one. Please feel free to send me any remarks good, bad and maybe indifferent.

I wish you the best of luck on your journey of learning.

Satash Singh

Table of Contents

DAY 1

Understand how to count

Shoonya	Zero	**Shoon ya**
Ek	One	**Ek**
Do	Two	**Do**
Teen	Three	**Teen**
Chaar	Four	**Chaar**
PaaNch	Five	**PaaNch**
Chhe	Six	**Chhe**
Saat	Seven	**Saat**
Aath	Eight	**Aath**
Nau	Nine	**Nau**
Das	Ten	**Das**
Gyaaraah	Eleven	**Gyaa raah**
Barah	Twelve	**Ba rah**
Terah	Thirteen	**Te rah**
Chaudah	Fourteen	**Chau dah**
Pandrah	Fifteen	**Pan drah**
Solah	Sixteen	**So lah**
Satrah	Seventeen	**Sat rah**
Athaarah	Eighteen	**Ath aa rah**
Unsath	Nineteen	**Un sath**
Bees	Twenty	**Bees**
Ikkees	Twenty one	**Ik kees**
Baaees	Twenty two	**Baa ee s**
Teees	Twenty three	**Te ees**
Chaubees	Twenty four	**Chau bees**
Pachchees	twenty five	**Pach chees**
Chhabbees	twenty six	**Chhab bees**
Sattaaees	twenty seven	**Sat taa ees**
ATTHaaees	twenty eight	**AT Thaa ees**
Untees	twenty nine	**Un tees**
Tees	Thirty	**Tees**
Ikattees	Thirty one	**Ikat tees**
Battees	Thirty two	**Bat tees**
TaiNttees	Thirty three	**TaiNt tees**
ChauNtees	Thirty four	**ChauN tees**

PaiNtees	Thirty five	**Pain tees**
Chaattees	Thirty six	**Chaat tees**
SaiNttees	Thirty seven	**SaiNt tees**
Artees	Thirty eight	**Ar tees**
Untaalees	Thirty nine	
Chaalees	Forty	**chaa lees**
Iktaalees	Forty one	**ik taa lees**
PaiNtaalees	Forty five	**Pain taa lees**
Bayaalees	Fortry two	**Ba yaa lees**
TaiNtaalees	Forty three	**PaiN taa lees**
Chavaalees	Forty four	**cha vaa lees**
Chhayaalees	Forty six	**chha yaa lees**
SaiNtaalees	Forty seven	**saiN taa lees**
Artaalees	Forty eight	**AR taa lees**
Unchaas	Forty nine	**Un chaas**
Pachaas	Fifty	**Pa chaas**
ikyaavan	Fifty one	**Ik yaa van**
Baavan	Fifty two	**Baa van**
Tirpan	Fifty three	**Tir pan**
Chauvan	Fifty four	**Chau van**
Pachpan	Fifty five	**Pach pan**
Chhappan	Fifty six	**Chap pan**
Sattaavan	Fifty seven	**Sat taa van**
ATTHaavan	Fifty eight	**AT Thaa va n**
UnsaTH	Fifty nine	**Un saTH**
SaaTH	Sixty	**SaaTH**
IksaTH	Sixty one	**Ik saTH**
BaasaTH	Sixty two	**Baa saTH**
TirsaTH	Sixty three	**Tir saTH**
ChauNsaTH	Sixty four	**ChauN saTH**
PaiNsaTH	Sixty five	**PaiN saTH**
ChhiyaasaTH	Sixty six	**Chhi yaa saTH**
SaRsaTH	Sixty seven	**Sar saTH**
ARsaTH	Sixty eight	**AR saTh**
Unhattar	Sixty nine	**Un hat tar**
Sattar	Seventy	**Sat tar**
Ikahattar	Seventy one	**I ka hat tar**
Bahattar	seventy two	**Ba hat tar**
Ti hat tar	seventy three	**Ti hat tar**
Chauhattar	Seventy four	**Chau hat tar**
Pachahattar	Seventy five	**Pa cha hat tar**
Chhihattar	seventy six	**Chhi hat tar**
Satahattar	seventy seven	**Sa ta hat tar**
ATHahattar	Seventy eight	**A THa hat tar**
Unaasee	Seventy nine	**U naa see**

Assee	Eighty	**As see**
Ikyaasee	Eighty one	**Ik yaa see**
Bayaasee	Eighty two	**Ba yaa see**
Tiraasee	Eighty three	**Ti raa see**
Chauraasee	Eighty four	**Chau raa see**
Pachaasee	Eighty five	**Pa chaa see**
Chhiyaasee	Eighty six	**Chhi yaa see**
Sataasee	Eighty seven	**Sa taa see**
ATTHaasee	Eighty eight	**AT Thaa see**
Navaasee	Eighty nine	**Na vaa see**
Nabbe	Ninety	**Nab be**
Ikyaanve	Ninety one	**Ik yaan ve**
Baanve	Ninety two	**Baan ve**
Tiraanve	Ninety three	**Ti raan ve**
Chauraanve	Ninety four	**Chau raan ve**
Pachaanve	Ninety five	**Pa chaan ve**
Chhiyaanve	Ninety six	**Chhi yaan ve**
Sattaanve	Ninety seven	**Sat taan ve**
ATTHaanve	Ninety eight	**AT THaan ve**
Ninyaanve	Ninety nine	**Nin yaan ve**
Sau	Hundred	**S au**
Ek haazaar	One thousand	**Ek haa zaar**
(Ek) laakh	One hundred thousand	**Laakh**
Das laakh	One million	**Das laakH**
(Ek) karoR	ten million	**Ka roR**
(Ek) Arab	One billion	**A rab**

DAY 2

Days of the week Hafte ke saat din

Ravivaar	Sunday	**Ravi vaar**
Itvaar	Sunday	**It vaar**
Somvaar	Monday	**Som vaar**
MaNgalvaar	Tuesday	**MaN gal vaar**
Budhvaar	Wednesday	**Budh vaar**
Guruvaar	Thursday	**Guru vaar**
Britaspativaar	Thursday	**Bri tas pati vaar**
Shukravaar	Friday	**Shuk ra vaar**
Shanivaar	Saturday	**Sha ni vaar**

Day and Night Raat aur Din

Din	Day	**Din**
Dopahar	Afternoon	**Do pa har**
Shaam	Evening dusk	**Sha am**
Subah	Morning dawn	**Su bah**
Aadhee raat	Midnight	**Aa dhee raat**
Raat	Night	**Raat**

Seasons RitueN

Garmee	Summer	**Gar mee**
Greeshm	Summer	**Gree shm**
Vaarshaa	Rains, monsoon	**Vaar shaa**
Barsaat	Rains, monsoon	**Bar saat**
Sharad	Autumn	**Sha rad**
PatjhaR	Autumn	**Pat jha R**
Shishir	Cool season	**Shi shir**

Hemant	Winter	**He mant**
Sardee	Winter	**Sar dee**
Basant	Spring	**Ba sant**

Colours RaNg

Peelaa	Yellow	**Pee laa**
Gulaabee	Pink	**Gu laa bee**
Haraa	Green	**Ha raa**
Jaamunee	Purple	**Jaa munee**
Kaalaa	Black	**Kaa laa**
Laal	Red	**Laal**
NaaraNgee	Orange	**Naa raN gee**
Neelaa	Blue	**Nee laa**
SaleTee	Grey	**Sa le tee**
Bhooraa	Brown	**Bhoo raa**
Safed	White	**Sa fed**

Parts of the body

Baal	Hair	**Baal**
AaNkh	Eye	**AaN kh**
Maathaa	Forehead	**Maa thaa**
Naak	Nose	**Na ak**
MuNh	Mouth	**Mu Nh**
ThoRee	Chin	**Tho ree**
Gaal	Cheek	**Ga al**
Kaan	Ear	**Ka an**
Eree	Heel	**E ree**
Pair kaa aNgooTHaa	Big toe	**Pa ir kaa aN goo Thaa**
Pair kee uNglee	Toe	**Pa ir kee uNg lee**
AngooTHaa	Thumb	**An goo Thaa**
Unglee	Finger	**Ung lee**
Naakhoon	Nail	**Naa khoon**
Sir	Head	**Sir**
Pee TH	Back	**Pee TH**
Kamar	Waist	**Ka mar**
JaaNgh	Thigh	**JaaN gh**
TaaNg	Leg	**Taa Ng**
GhuTnaa	Knee	**GhuT naa**

PeT	Stomach	**P eT**
Kuhnee	Elbow	**Kuh nee**
Kohnee	Elbow	**Koh nee**
BaaNh	Arm	**Baa Nh**
Baajoo	Arm	**Baa joo**

Family members Rishtedaar

Pitaa	Father	**Pi taa**
Maataa	Mother	**Maa taa**
Bahin	Sister	**Ba hin**
Bahan	Sister	**Ba han**
Bhaaee	Brother	**Bha aee**
Bahnoee	Brother-in-law	**Bah no ee**
Bhaabhee	Sister-in-law	**Bhaa bhee**
BhaaNjaa	Sister's son	**BhaaN jaa**
BhaaNjee	Sister's daughter	**BhaaN jee**
Bhateejaa	Brother's son	**Bha tee jaa**
Bhateejee	Brother's daughter	**Bha tee jee**
Pati	Husband	**Pa ti**
Patnee	Wife	**Pat nee**
Betaa	Son	**Be taa**
BeTee	Daughter	**Be tee**
Bahoo	Daughter-in-law	**Ba hoo**
Daamaad	Son-in-law	**Daa maad**
Potaa	Grandson (son's son)	**Po taa**
Potee	Granddaughter (son's Daughter)	**Po tee**
Naatee	Grandson (daughter's son)	**naa tee**
Naatin	Granddaughter (daughter's daughter)	**Naa tin**
Daadaa	Paternal grandfather	**Daa daa**
Daadee	Paternal grandmother	**Daa dee**
Buaa	Father's sister	**Bu aa**
Foofaa	Fathers sister's husband	**Foo faa**
Chaachaa	Fathers younger brother	**Chaa chaa**
Chaachee	Fathers younger brother wife	**Chaa chee**
Taau	Father older brother	**Ta au**
Taaee	Father older brother wife	**Taa ee**
Sasur	Father-in-law	**Sa sur**
Saas	Mother-in-law	**Sa as**
Saalaa	Wife's brother	**Saa laa**

Saalee	Wife's sister	**Saa lee**
Salhaj	Wife's brother's wife	**Sal haj**
Saarhoo	Wife's sister husband	**Saar hoo**
Naanaa	Maternal grandmother	**Naa naa**
Naanee	Maternal grandfather	**Naa nee**
Maasee	Mothers sister	**Maa see**
Mausaa	Mother sister husband	**Mau saa**
Maamaa	Mother brother	**Maa maa**
Maamee	Mother brother wife	**Maa mee**
Nanad	Husbands sister	**Na nad**
Nandoee	Husband sister husband	**Nan do ee**
Devar	Husband younger brother	**De var**
Devraanee	Husbands younger brother wife	**Dev raan ee**
JeTH	Husbands older brother	**Je TH**
JeTHaanee	Husbands older brother wife	**Je TH aa nee**

DAY 3

Foods and beverage Khaane-peene kee cheezeN

Dahee	Yogurt	**Da hee**
Paneer	Cottage cheese	**Pan eer**
Besam	Flour	**Bes am**
AaTaa	Flour	**Aa taa**
Chaaval	Rice	**Chaa val**
Cheenee	Sugar	**Chee nee**
GehooN	Wheat	**Ge hooN**
Khajoor	Date	**Kha joor**
Haldee	Tumeric	**Hal dee**
Imlee	Tamarind	**Im lee**
Supaaree	Betel nut	**Su paa ree**
Namak	Salt	**Na mak**
Kaalee mirch	Black pepper	**Kaa lee mir ch**
Tel	Oil	**T el**
Masaale	Spices	**Ma saa le**
Daal	Lentils pulses	**D aal**
Mirch	Pepper, chilli's	**Mir ch**
Dalbalro Tee	Bread	**Dal bal ro tee**
Doodh	Milk	**Doo dh**
Makkhan	Butter	**Mak kh an**
Kaufee	Coffee	**Kau fee**
ANDe	Eggs	**AN De**
Paanee	Water	**Paa nee**
Shahad	Honey	**Sha had**
Chaay	Tea	**Ch aay**
Kishmish	Raisin	**Kish mish**
Baadaam	Almonds	**Baa daam**
Pistaa	Pistachio	**Pis taa**
AkhroT	Walnut	**A kh roT**
Kaajoo	Cashew nut	**Kaa joo**

Fruit Phal

Kelaa	Banana	Ke laa
Seb	Apple	S eb
Santraa	Orange	San tra a
Aam	Mango	A am
Shareefaa	Custard apple	Sha ree faa
Mausmee	Grapefruit	Maus mee
AaRoo	Peach	Aa Roo
LaukaaT	Nectarine	Lau kaaT
Naashpaatee	Pear	Naa sh paa tee
Amrood	Guava	Am rood
Rasbharee	Raspberry	Ras bha ree
Angoor	Grapes	An goor
Strauberee	Strawberry	Strau be ree
Cheree	Cherry	Che ree
Anannaas	Pineapple	An ann aas
Naariyal	Coconut	Naa ri yal
Aaloobukhaaraa	Plum	Aa loo bu khaa raa
Tarbooj	Watermelon	Tar booj
Tarbooz	Watermelon	Tar booz
Papeeta	Papaya	Pa pee ta
Kharbooja	Musk melon	Khar boo ja
Anaar	Pomegranate	An aar

Vegetables SabziyaaN

Khumbee	Mushroom	Khum bee
Kachaaloo	Esculent root	Ka chaa loo
Aaloo	Potato	Aa loo
Ma Tar	Peas	Ma tar
Pyaaz	Onions	Pya az
Shalgam	Turnip	Shal gam
TinDaa	Squash	Tin Daa
BaiNgan	Eggplant	BaiN gan
Karelaa	Bitter squash	Ka re laa
Adrak	Ginger	Ad rak

Kaddoo	Pumpkin	**Kad doo**
Gaajaar	Carrot	**Gaa jaar**
Toree	Ribbed squash	**To ree**
Moolee	Radish	**Moo lee**
Phoolgobhee	Cauliflower	**Phool go bhee**
Chukandar	Beetroot	**Chu kan dar**
Bandgobhee	Cabbage	**Band go bhee**
Kheerah	Cucumber	**Khee rah**
Neeboo	Lemon	**Nee boo**
Neemboo	Lemon	**Neem boo**
BhinDee	Okra, lady finger	**Bhin dee**
Tamaa Tar	Tomato	**Ta maa tar**
PhaliyaaN	Bean	**Pha li yaaN**

Birds Panchchee

Giddh	Vulture	**Gid dh**
Ulloo	Owl	**Ul loo**
Baaz	Eagle	**Ba az**
Kauaa kauvaa	Crow	**Kau aa kau vaa**
Koyal	Cuckoo	**Ko yal**
Papeeha	Cuckoo	**Pa pee ha**
Mainah	Mynah	**Mai nah**
Batakh	Duck	**Ba takh**
Kabootar	Pigeon	**Ka boo tar**
ChiRiyaa	Sparrow	**ChiR i yaa**
Totaa	Parrot	**To taa**

Animals Jaanvar

Titlee	Butterfly	**Tit lee**
MakRee	Spider	**Mak ree**
Makkhee	Fly	**Mak khee**
MeNDHak	Frog	**MeN Dhak**
Chhipkalle	Lizard	**Chhip kal le**
Choohaa	Rat, Mouse	**Choo haa**
GirgiT	Garden lizard	**Gir giT**
Naag	Cobra	**Na ag**
Nevlaa	Mongoose	**Nev laa**

Ajgar	Python	**Aj gar**
Bakree	Goat	**Bak ree**
Bhaaloo	Bear	**Bhaa loo**
Kutta	Dog	**Kut ta**
BhaiNs	Buffalo	**Bha I Ns**
Gadhaa	Donkey	**Ga dha a**
Ghoraa	Horse	**Gho raa**
Jiraaf	Giraffe	**Ji ra af**
LakkaR harnaa	Giraffe	**Lak kaR har naa**
Magarmachch	Crocodile	**Ma gar ma ch ch**
Machhlee	Fish	**Ma chh lee**
Bandar	Monkey	**Ban dar**
Gilahree	Squirrel	**Gi lah ree**
Khargosh	Rabbit, Hare	**Khar gosh**
ChamgaadaR	Bat	**Cham gaa daR**
GeedaR	Jackal	**Gee daR**
LomRee	Fox	**Lom Ree**
BaarahsiNgaa	Stag	**Baa rah siN gaa**
Baagh	Tiger	**Baa gh**
Sher	Lion	**Sh er**

DAY 4

Greetings

How are you

Aap kaise haiN?

How are you?

Tum kaise ho?

How are you?

Tum kaisee ho?

How are you?

Ye kaisaa hi?

How is he/it?

Ye kaise hi

How are they?

Vo kaisaa hi

How is it/he?

Vo kaisee hi

How is she/it?

Ve kaise haiN

How are they?

How are they?

Pitaajee kaise haiN?

How is father

Ve THeek haiN
He is fine

Tumaaree maataajee kaisee haiN
How is your mother

Ve bhee THeek haiN
She is also fine

Tumaaree bahineN kaisee haiN
How is your sisters

Ve achchhee haiN
They are fine

Tumaaree bhaaee haiN
How are your brothers

They are well

Ve THeek haiN
They are fine

Ve kaise haiN
How are/is they/he

Ve THeek haiN
They/he are/is fine

Vo kaisee hai
How is she

Vo bilkul THeek hai
She is absolutely fine

Vo kaisaa hai

How is he

Vo beemaar hai

He is ill

Ve kaisee haiN

How are/is they/he

Ve maze maiN haiN

They/he are/is having fun

Ve THeek naheeN haiN

They/he are/is not well

Formal

Aapke haalchaal haiN

How are you

Aapkee meharbaanee hai

It is your kindness/grace

Aapkee duaa se THeek haiN

By your prayers, I am fine

Aapkee mizaaj kaise haiN

How are you

Aap kaise haiN

How are you

Ham THeek haiN

I am fine

Ham bilkul THeek haiN

We are absolutely fine

DAY 5

Pronouns

LaRkee kaisee hai

How is the girl

Vo THeek hai

She is fine

LaRkaa kaisaa hai

How is the boy

Vo THeek haiN

He is fine

LaRkiyaaN kaisee haiN

How are the girls

Ve achchhe haiN

They are fine

LaRke kaise haiN

How are the boys

BahueN kaisee haiN

How are the daughters-in-law

Bahoo kaisee hai

How is the daughter-in-law

MaiN paRhtaa thaa

I (mas) used to read/study

MaiN paRhtee thee

I (fem) used to read/study

Too paRhtaa thaa

You (mas) used to read

Too paRhtee thee

You (fem) used to read

Ye likhta thaa

He used to write

Ye likhtee thee

She used to write

Vo likhtaa thaa

He used to write

Vo likhtee thee

She used to write

Ye gaataa thaa

He used to sing

Ye gaatee thee

She used to sing

Vo gaataa thaa

He used to sing

Vo gaatee thee

She used to sing

Ham paRhte the

We (mas) used to read

Ham paRhtee theeN
We (fem) used to read

Tum paRhte the
You (mas) used to read

Tum paRhtee theeN
You (fem) used to read

PaRhnaa
Read
Likhnaa
Write
Gaanaa
Sing

At the airport

MaiN havaaee jahaaz meN aayaa
I flew in an airoplane

Ye havaaee aDDa hai
This is the airport

Meera saamaan kahaaN se milegaa
Where will I get my luggage

Ye meraa passporT hai
Here is my passport

Vimaan kee hosTess achchhee thee
This air hostess is good

PaailaT hamse baar kar rahaa thaa
The pilot was talking to us

DAY 6

I will

MaiN jaaooNgaa

I (masculine) will go

MaiN jaaooNgee

I (feminine) will go

too jaaegaa

You (masculine) will go

Too jaaegee

You (feminine) will go

Ye rukegaa

He will stop/stay

Ye rukegee

She will stop/stay

Vo rukegaa

He will stop/stay

Vo rukegee

She will stop/stay

Ye bolegaa

He will speak

Ye bolegee

She will speak

Vo bolegaa

He will speak

Vo bolegee

She will speak

Jaanaa

To go

Ruknaa

To stop

Bolnaa

To talk

We will

Ham jaaeNge

We (masculine) will go

Ham jaaeNgee

We (feminine) will go

tum jaaoge

You (masculine) will go

Tum jaaogee

You (feminine) will go

Tum rukoge

You (masculine) will stop

Tum rukogee

You (feminine) will stop

Aap rukeNge	You (masculine) will stop
Aap rukeNgee	You (feminine) will stop
Aap boleNge	You (masculine) will speak
Aap boleNgee	You (feminine) will speak
Ye boleNge	He/they will speak
Ye boleNgee	She/they will speak

DAY 7

Shiv and Simi will

Shiv vahaaN jaaegaa
Shiv will go there

Simi vahaaN jaaegee
Simi will go there

Shiv aur Simi vahaaN jaaeNge
Shiv and Simi will go there

Lalita aur Simi vahaaN jaaeNgee
Lalita and Simi will go there

Simi khaaegee
Simi will eat

Shiv aur Simi hkaaeNge
Shiv and Simi will eat

Lalita aur Simi hkaaeNgee
Lalita and Simi will eat

Shiv aur Amit hkaaeNge
Shiv and Amit will eat

Shiv gaanaa sunegaa
Shiv will listen to a song

Simi gaanaa sunegee
Simi will listen to a song

Shiv aur Simi gaanaa suneNge
Shiv and Simi will listen to a song

Lalita aur Simi gaanaa suneNgee
Lalita and Simi will listen to a song

Shiv aur shyaam gaana suneNge
Shiv and shyam will listen to a song

Gaanaa
Song

Jaanaa
To go

Khaanaa
To eat

Travel

Ham haavaaee jahaz se aae haiN
We have come by airplane

Ham haavaaee aDDa se taiksee leNge
We will take a taxi from the airport

Ham relgaaRee se aae haiN
We have come by train

Ham relve sTeshan se taiksee leNge
We will take a taxi from the railway station

Ham bas se aae haiN
We have come by bus

Ham bas aDDe se taiksee leNge
We will take a taxi from the bus stand

Modes of transport

MaiN taiksee se jaaooNgee
I (feminine) will go by taxi

MaiN auto-rikshaa se aaooNgee
I (feminine) will come by auto-rickshaa

MaiN three-veelar aaooNgee
I (feminine) will come by auto-rickshaa

MaiN rikshaa se aaooNgee
I (feminine) will come by auto-rickshaa

MaiN bas se jaaooNgee
I (feminine) will come by bus

MaiN kaar se jaaooNgee
I (feminine) will go by/in a car

MaiN kaar meN jaaooNgee
I (feminine) will go by/in a car

MaiN skooTar se aaooNgee
I (feminine) will come by/on a skooter

DAY 8

Directions

Timehri dakshiN: Ghayaanaa meN hai
Timehri is in south Guyana

Lethem uttar Ghayaanaa meN hai
Lethem is in north Guyana

Lenora pashchim Ghayaanaa meN hai
Lenora is in west Guyana

Mahaica poorva Ghayaana meN hai
Mahaica is in east Guyana

DakshiN
South

Uttar
North

Pashchim
West

Poorva
East

Distances

Ye jagah door hai
This place is far

Ye jagah paas hai
This place is nearby

Ye jagah naazdeek hai
This place is nearby

Ye jagah bahut paas hai
This place is very near

Ye jagah bahut kareeb hai
This place is very near

Ye jagah bahut door hai
This place is very far

Door
Far

Nazdeek
Near

Paas
Near

Bahut kareeb
Very near

Distances

Amit yahaaN se daaeN muRegaa
Amit will turn right from here

Amit vahaaN se baaeN muRegaa
Amit will turn left from there

Amit sTeshan ke paas jaaegaa
Amit will past near the (bus) station

Amit mandir ke peechhe se jaaegaa

Amit will go from behind the temple

Amit aglee galee se seedhaa jaaegaa

Amit will go straight from the next lane

DaaeN

Right

BaaeN

Left

Paas

Near

Ke peechhe

Behind

Seedhaa

Straight

Cardinal numbers

MaiN ek ghoRaa hooN

I am one/a horse

Ham do bandar haiN

We two monkeys

Ye teen bhaaloo haiN

These are three bears

Ham chaar bakriyaaN haiN

We are four goats

Ye paaNche kachhue haiN

These are five tortoises

Ham chhe billiyaaN haiN

We are six cats

Ye saat khargosh haiN
These are seven rabbits

Ham aaTH tote haiN
We are eight parrots

Ye nau choohe haiN
These are nine mice

Ham das kauve Hain
We are ten crows

Suppositions

Tum achchhe kaam karte to tumheN sab pyaar karte
If you had done good deeds, everyone would have loved you

Aap chaate to bahut kuchh kar sakte the
If you had wanted to, you could have done a lot

Tum thoRee der pahle aa jaate to vo tumheN mil jaataa
If you had come a little earlier, you could have met him

Agar tumne kal kahaa hotaa to ham aaj tumhaaraa saamaan le aarte
If you had mentioned it yesterday, we would have brought your things today

Tumne ye khabar kal dee hotee, to zyaadaa achchhaa hotaa
If you had given us this news yesterday, it would have been better

Ham Aagraa navambar meN gae hote, to mausam zyaadaa suhaavnaa hotaa
If we had gone to agra in November, the weather would have been better

DAY 9

Occasion of holi

Hamne naachtaa huaa mor dekhaa
We saw a dancing peacock

uRte hue panchhee bahut sundar lagte haiN
Flying birds look beautiful

Chalte-chalte maiN apne ghar pahuNch gayaa
Walking I reach my home

Naachte-naachte Simi gir gaee
Simi fell while dancing

Kahaanee sunaate hue vo ro paRee
While telling the story she burst into tears

Baat karte hue vo haNsne lagaa
He started laughing while talking

Gire hue peR par ek ghoNslaa thaa
There was a nest on the fallen tree

Jalee hue lakree kee raakh pheNk do
Throw away the ash of the burnt wood

Tum baiTHe-baiTHe bor naheen ho rahe
Aren’t you getting bored sitting like this

Dhule kapRoN ko andar le aao
Bring the washed clothes inside

Beetee baatoN ko bhool jaanaa chaahie
You should forget the past

Zameen par paRe kaagaz ko kooRedaan meN Daalo
Throw the paper laying on the floor in the dust bin

Holee jalaane ke lie lakRee kahaaN hai
Where is the wood to burn the Holi

Paanee meN raNg ghol do
Dissolve the colour in the water

Baazaar se gulaal laao
Get some dry colour from the market

gubaaroN meN raNg vaalaa paanee bharo
Fill the ballons with coloured water

Meree pichkaaree laao
Get my water pump

Aao, ham gujhiyaa khaaeN
Come we will eat some gujhiya

Chalo, sabse holee milke aaeN
Come, lets go and greet everybody on holi

DAY 10

Conditional

Agar Shiv aae to use mere paas bhejnaa
If Shiv comes send him to me

Agar Amit daftar jaa rahaa ho to mujhe bhee saath le jaae
If Amit is going to the office, he should take me along

Simi tumheN kuchh kahe to mujhe bataanaa
If Simi says anything to you, let me know

Deedee tumse laRe to use mere paas le aanaa
if your elder sister fights with you, bring her to me

Agar Shiv meree kitaab laaegaa to maiN use uskee kitaab dhooNgee
If Shiv brings my book, I will give him his book

Simi yahaaN aaegaa to ham baazaar jaaeNge
If Simi comes here, we will go to the market

Vela der se aaee mujhse daaNT khaaeegee
If Vela comes late, she will get a scolding from me

Animals

Hamne jaNgal meN sher dekhaa
We saw a lion in the jungle

Hamne chiRiyaaghar meN haathee dekhe
We saw elephants in the zoo

Hamne zoo meN bahut-se jaanvar dekhe
We saw lots of animals in the zoo

Hamne jaNgal meN baagh dekhaa
We saw a tiger in the jungle

Hamne jaNgal meN hiran dekhaa
We saw a deer in the jungle

Hamne cheRyaaghar meN saaNp dekhe
We saw snakes in the jungle

Hamne zoo meN magarmachchh dekhe
We saw crockodiles in the zoo

Hamne jaNgal meN Bhaaloo dekhaa
We saw a bear in the jungle

Birds

jaNgal meN panchhee chahak rahe the
The birds were chirping in the jungle

Zoo meN mor naach rahaa thaa
A peacock was dancing in the zoo

Hamne batakh ko daanaa khilaayaa
We fed the duck

Hamne bahut saare tote dekhe
We saw many parrots

Hamne ek baRee cheel dekhee
We saw a big kite

Koyal ke aavaaz bahut mee THee hotee hai
The cuckoo has a very sweat voice

Kabootar bahut Darpok hotaa hai
The pigeon is very timid

Shaturmurg bahut baRaa hotaa hai
The ostrich is very large

DAY 11

Visiting a doctor, Common ailments

Meraa galaa kharaab hai

I have a soar throat

Mere sir meN dard hai

I have a head ache

Mere peT meN dard hai

I have a stomach ache

Mere pairoN meN dard hai

My feet is aching

Use khaaNsee hai

He/she have a cough

Use bukhaar hai

He/she have a fever

Use choT lag gaee hai

He/she is hurt

Use THanD lag gaee hai

He/she has catch a cold

Use zukaam hai

He/she have a cold

Serious ailments

Use malariaa ho gayaa hai
He/she has caught malaria

Use dil kaa dauraa paRaa hai
He/she had a heart attack

Use joRoN meN bahut dard hai
He/she have a lot of pain in the joints

Use ulTiyaaN aa rahee haiN
He/she is vomiting

Uske haath meN fraikchar ho gayaa hai
He/she has fractured his/her hand

Use pair kee haDDee TooT gaee hai
He/she has broken a bone of the foot

Remedies

daakTar saahab ko jaldee se fon karo
Telephone the doctor quickly

Use injekshan lagaanaa hogaa
We will have to give her/him an injection

Use ye goliyaaN aur kaipsool dene hai
He/she has to be given these tablets and capsules

Use fauran aspataal meN bhartee karvaanaa chaahie
We should admit him/her to the hospital immediately

Use aaShiv karnaa chaahie
He/she should take a test

Use ye davaaee do
Give him/her this medicine

Use choT par paTTe baandh do
Bandage his/her wound

Vo kuchh din meN THeek ho jaaegaa
He/she will be alright in a few days

DAY 12

Days weeks months

Ham somvaar ko khaanaa naheeN khaate
We do not eat on Mondays

Janvaree meN dillee meN bahut THanD hotee hai
In January, it is very cold in delhi

Shiv maNgalvaar ko mandir jaataa hai
Shiv goes to the temple on Tuesdays

Agle hafte mere paas bahut kaam hai
I have a lot of work to do next week

Pichhle hafte meree chhuTTiyyaan theeN
I had holidays last week

Hole maarch meN aatee hai
Holi is in march

Asking the time

ghaRee meN kyaa bajaa hai
What is the time in the watch

Samay kyaa huaa hai
What is the time

Vakt kyaa huaa hai

What is the time

Meree ghaRee meN chhe baje haiN
It is six o'clock according to my watch

Is samay THeek das baje haiN
It is now exactly ten o'clock

naaTak THeek aaTH baje shuru hogaa
The play will start at eight o'clock sharp

Vo das baje kea as-paas aaegaa
He will come around ten o'clock

Abhee tren chhoThe meN aadhaa ghanTaa hai
There is half an hour to go before the train leaves

Shiv yahaaN se paunaa ghanTaa chalaa gayaa
Shiv left here 45 minutes ago

Simi savaa ghanTe meN aaegee
Simi will come here in quarter of an hour

DAY 13

Should and ought to

Mujhe ab jaanaa chaahie
I should go now

tumheN maaN ko roz ek chiTTHee likhnee chaahie
You should write a letter to mother everyday

tumheN khaanaa banaanaa seekhnaa chaahie
You should learn to cook food

Mujhe pitaajee se aise naheeN bonaa chaahie thaa
I ought not to have spoken to father like this

Aapko vahaaN zaroor jaanaa chaahie
You should certainly go there

Tumhaaraa yahaaN aanaa bahut zarooree hai
It is very important that you come here

Must and have to

Shiv ko ye kaam karnaa hee hogaa
Shiv will have to do this work

Aaj tumheN baazaar jaanaa paRegaa
Today you will have to go to the market

Mujhe aaj apnaa kamraa saaf karnaa paRegaa
I will have to clean my room today

Use kal maaseejee ke ghar jaanaa hai
He/she has to go to aunt's house tomorrow

tumheN parsoN apne dostoN se milne jaanaa hai
You have to go and meet your friends the day after tomorrow

hameN use milne jaanaa hogaa
We will have to go and meet him/her

Had and come

Shiv pichhle maheene yahaa Naayaa thaa
Shiv had come here last month

Amit agle maheene yahaaN aaegaa
Amit will come here next month

Anand kal yahaaN aaee thee
Anand had come here yesterday

Ravi parsoN yahaaN aaee thee
Ravi had come here the day before yesterday

Sandra kal yahaaN aaegee

Sandra will come here tomorrow

Rick parsoN yahaaN aaegaa
Rick will come here the day after tomorrow

Shaun agle saal yahaaN aaegaa
Shaun will come next year

Ham agle maheene apne gaaNv jaa rahe haiN
We are going to our village next month

DAY 14

Ki as in that

main chaahtaa hooN ki tum bahut tarakkee karo
I want that you should progress a lot

main dekh rahaa hooN ki aajkal tum bilkul naheeN paRh rahe
I see that you are not studying at all these days

Main soch rahaa hooN ki ek naee gaaRee khareedee jaae
I am thinking that a new car should be bought

Simi ko laagaa ki Shiv aayaa hai
It seemed to seta that Shiv had come

maiNne paRhaa thaa ki haathee kee yaaddaasht bahut tez hotee hai
I had read that the elephant have a sharp memory

maiNne sunaa hai ki naTvarlaal ek THag hai
I have read that natvarlal is a cheat

Using "jo"

Jo mainNe sunaa, kyaa vo sach hai
Is what I have heard true

Vahee karo jo Shiv bataa rahaa hai

Do whatever Shiv is telling you

hameN jo chaahie, vo is dukaanmeN naheeN hai
What we want is not available in this shop

Kal jo kitaab main le gaee thee, vo gum gaee
I lost the book that I had taken yesterday

Tum jo kaam kar rahe ho, vo galat hai
What you are doing is wrong

Jo aadmee kal yahaaN aayaa thaa, kyaa tum use jaantaa ho
Do you know the man who came here yesterday

"Se par" after "jo"

Jisse tum baat kar rahee theeN, vo hamaaree naee paRosan hai
The person you were talking to is our new neighbour

Tumne jise ghar bulaayaa hai, kyaa maiN use jaantee hooN
Do I know the person you have invited home

Mujhe vo mez chaahie jispar kapRe paRe haiN
I want the table on which the clothes are lying

Jis kitaab ko tumne gumaayaa hai, use DHooNDHo
Look for the book you have lost

Jise tumne gumaayaa hai us kitaab ko DHooNDHo
Look for the book you have lost

Ye kitaab jiskee hai, use yahaaN bulaao
Call the person whose book this is

"Ne" after "jo"

Shiv ko jonhoNne bulaayaa hai, ve mere pitaajee haiN
The person who has called Shiv is my father

Tumse jisne baat kee thee, vo meree bahan hai
The person who had spoken to you is my sister

Jisne Simi ko ye saamaan diyaa thaa, vo kahaaN hai
Where is the person who have given Simi these things

jinhoNne hamse kitaabeN khareedee theeN, unhoNne paise naheeN die
The people who have bought these books from us have not yet paid the money

Jisne haamaaraa ghar khareedaa hai, vo ek DaukTar hai
The person who have bought our house is a doctor

DAY 15

Whoever whatever

Jo bhee tumse ye khaTaaraa gaaRee khareedegaa, vo saaree zindagee roegaa

Whoever buys this wrecked car from you will cry for the rest of his life

Jo kuchh tum kah rahe ho, vo sab bakvaas hai

What you are saying is all nonsense

Jo kuchh tumne sunaa hai, vo sab jhooTH hai

Whatever you have heard is false

Jo bhee tum laae ho, vo sab us kamre meN rakhaa hai

Whatever you have bought is kept in that room

At a wedding

Maala kee shaadee anil se hogee

Maala will get married to Anil

Baaraat raat ko aaegee

The wedding will take place at night

Maala dulhan hai

Mala is the bride

Anil doolhaa hai
Anil is the bridegroom

Maala kee dolee subah jaaegee
Maala "doll" will leave in the morning

Ornaments

Dulhan ko chooRiyaaN pahnaao
Put bangles on the bride

Dulhan ko haar pahnaao
Put a necklace on the bride

Dulhan ko aNgoo Thee pahnaao
Put a ring on the bride

Dulhan ko paayaal pahnaao
Put anklets on the bride

Dulhan kaa nath laao
Bring the brides nosepin

Dulhan ko bindee lagaao
Put a bindee on the bride forehead

Dulhan ko maaNgTeekaa pahnaao
Put a marriage band on the bride

Dulhan ko jhumke pahnaao
Put earrings on the bride

Dulhan ka mangalsootra laao
Bring the brides marriage band

DAY 16

Bigger biggest

Lalita Simi se baRee hai
Lalita is older than Simi

Shiva sabse baRee hai
Shiv is the eldest

Shiv Lalita se ooNchaa hai
Shiv is higher than Lalita

maaunT EvaresT sabse ooNchaa hai
Mount Everest is the highest

Britain Guyana se baRaa hai
Britain is large than Guyana

Canada sabse baRaa hai
Canada is the largest

Baadshaah begam se baRaa hai
The king is bigger than the queen

Begam gulaam se baRee hai
The queen is bigger than the jack

Ikkaa sabse baRaa hai
The ace is the biggest

More less

Kaale joote safed jootoN se zyaadaa mahNge haiN
The black shoes are more expensive than the white one

Safed joote kaale jootoN se zyaadaa saste haiN
The white shoes are more expensive than the black one

Vo kitaab is kitaab se zyaadaa mahNge hai
That book is more expensive than that book

Ye kitaab us kitaab se zyaadaa sastee hai
This book is more cheap than that book

Kale joote zyaadaa mahNge haiN
The black shoes are more expensive

Safed joote kam mahNge haiN
The white shoes are less expensive

Vo kitaab zyaadaa mahNgee hai
That book is more expensive

Ye kitaab kam mahNgee hai
That book is less expensive

Like dislike

Mujhe ghoomnaa-phirnaa achchhaa logtaa hai
I like traveling

Mujhe khaanaa banaanaa achachhaa logtaa hai
I like cooking

Muje likhnaa achchhaa lagtaa hai
I like writing

Use ghoomnaa-phirnaa achachhaa naheeN lagtaa
He/she does not like traveling

Use khaanaa banaanaa naheeN achchhaa hai
He/she does not like to cook

Use likhnaa naheeN achchhaa hai
He/she does not like to write

Mujhe ghoomne-phirne kaa shauk hai
I like traveling

Mujhe khaanaa banaane kaa shauk hai
I like cooking

Mujhe likhne kaa shauk hai
I like writing

Use ghoomne-phirne se nafrat hai
He/she hates traveling

Use khaanaa banaane se nafrat hai
He/she hates cooking

Use likhne se nafrat hai
He/she hates writing

Achchaa

Like

Achchhaa nahin

Dislike

Shauk

Like

Nafrat

Dislike

DAY 17

At the bank

Vo paise jamaa karne kaa kaaunTar hai
That is the counter for depositing money

Ye paise nikaalne ka kaaunTar hai
That is the counter for withdrawing money

yahaaN chek jamaa hote haiN
Cheques are deposited here

vahaaN draaft bantaa hai
Drafts are made there

Jamaa
Receipts

Nikaalne
Payments

At the post office

vahaaN daak-TikaT milte haiN
Postage stamps are available here

Udhar manee-aurDar jamaa hotaa hai
Money-orders are deposited here

Idar lifaafe milte haiN
Envelopes are available here

Idhar se rajisTree bhejte haiN
Registered post is sent from here

yahaaN se speeD-posT hotaa hai
Speed post facility is available here

rajisTree
Registered
Bhejte
Sent
Daak-TikaT
Stamps
Lifaafe
Envelopes

DAY 18

Hobbies in and on

kapRe almaaree meN haiN	The clothes are in the cupboard
kapRe sandook meN haiN	The clothes are in the trunk
kapRe daraaz meN haiN	The clothes are in the drawer
kapRe baalTee meN haiN	The clothes are in the bucket
kapRe mez par haiN	The clothes are on the table
kapRe kursee par Hai	The clothes are on the chair
kapRe palaNg par haiN	The clothes are on the bed
Kapre zameen par haiN	The clothes are on the ground

Zameen	Ground
palaNg	Bed

Kursee
Chair
Mez
Table
baalTee
Bucket
Daraaz
Drawer
Sandook
Trunk
Almaaree
Cupboard

Where

Mujhe kamre ke baahar milnaa
See me outside the room

Mujhe haul ke andar milnaa
See me inside the hall

Mujhe chhat ke oopar milnaa
See me on the roof

Mujhe skool ke paas milnaa
See me near the school

Mujhe mandir ke peechhe milnaa
See me behind the temple

Mujhe dukaan ke aage milnaa
See me in front of the shop

Mujhe seeRhiyoN ke neeche milnaa
See me below the stairs

Mujhe hoTal ke saamne milnaa
See me in front of the hotel

With and without

Simi Shiv ke saath aaegee
Simi will come with Shiv

Simi Shiv kee jagah aaegee
Simi will come in place of Shiv

Simi Shiv ke bajaay aaegee
Simi will come instead of Shiv

Simi Shiv ke binaa aaegee
SImi will come without Shiv

Hobbies and interest

Mujhe laRnaa pasand hai
I like fighting

Mujhe kitaabeN paRhnaa pasand hai
I like reading books

Mujhe saNgeet kaa shauk hai
I like music

Mujhe nritya/naachne kaa shauk hai

I like dance/dancing

Mujhe khelne kaa shauk hai

I like playing

Mujhe T.V dekhnaa achchhaa lagtaa hai

I like watching TV

Mujhe baagbaanee karnaa pasand hai

I like gardening

Mujhe ghoomnaa-phirnaa achchhaa lagtaa hai

I like traveling roaming around

Mujhe khaane kaa shauk hai

I like eating

Mujhe sonaa pasand hai

I like sleeping

DAY 19

The sky

Aasmaan kitnaa sundar lag rahaa hai
How beautiful the sky seems

Aaj pooraa chaand khitaa hai
Today the moon is full

Chaandnee kitnee sundar hai
How beautiful the moon light is

Vo taaraa kaise charnak rahaa hai
How that star is twinkling

Kitnee THanDee havaa chal rahee hai
How cool the breeze is

Aakaash meN bahut kaale baadal haiN
The sky is overcast with black clouds

Bijlee chamak rahee hai
There is lightning

Baadal garaj rahe haiN
There is thunder

Baarish ho rahee hai
It is raining

Ole paR rahe haiN
There is hail storms

Ole
Hailstorm
Bearish
Rain
Baadal
Thunder
Bijlee
Lightening
Kaale baadal
Black clouds
THanDee havaa
Cool breeze
Taaraa
Star
Chaandnee
Moon

DAY 20

Adjectives

Ye sharbat THanDaa hai
The syrup is cold

Ye chaay THanDee hai
The tea is cold

Vo sharbat gaShiv hai
The syrup is hot

Vo chaay gaShiv hai
The tea is hot

Ye sharbat achchhaa hai
This syrup is good

Ye chaay achchhee hai
This tea is good

Vo sharbat baRhiyaa hai
This syrup is fine

Vo chaay baRhiyaa hai
This tea is fine

THanDaa
Cold

GaShiv
Hot

Achchhaa

Good

baRhiyaa

Fine

light, heavy and cheap

Ye palaNg halkaa hai

This bed is light

Ye kursee halkee hai

This chair is light

Ye palaNg halke haiN

These beds are light

Ye kursiyaaN halkee haiN

These chairs are light

Ye palaNg bhaaree hai

This bed is heavy

Ye kursee bhaaree hai

This chair is heavy

Ye palaNg bhaaree haiN

These beds are heavy

Ye kursiyaaN bhaaree haiN

These chairs are heavy

Ye palaNg sastaa hai

This bed is cheap

Ye kursee sastee hai
This chair is cheap

Ye palaNg saste HaiN
These beds are cheap

Ye kursiyaaN sastee haiN
These chairs are cheap

Halkaa
Light
Bhaaree
Heavy
Sastaa
Cheap

Nature

Ye bageeche kitne hare haiN
How green these gardens are

Ye phool kitne sundar haiN
How beautiful these flowers are

Is jheel kaa paanee kitnaa neelaa hai
How blue the water of this lake is

Is jharne kaa paanee kaise chamak rahaa hai
How that water falls is glittering

pahaaR kitne shaant lagte haiN
How peacefull the mountain seems

Is vaadee meN kitne peR haiN
How many trees are in this valley

Palaces

Aagraa kaa kilaa bahut aaleeshaan hai
Agra fort is really magnificent

Laal kilaa dillee meN hai
Red fort is in Dehli

Baadshaah humaayooN kaa makbaraa dillee meN hai
Emperor humayun's tomb is in Dehli

Lek pailes udaipur meN hai
Lake palace is in udaipur

Baadshaah akbar kaa makbaraa Sikandraa meN hai
Emperor Akbar tomb is in Sikandra

Mahaaraajaa umaid singh kaa mahal Jodhpur meN hai
King Umaid Singh palace is in Jodhpur

VOCABULARY

Aajkal	Nowadays
Aanaa	To come
Aap	You
Aapkaa	Your, yours
Achchhaa	Good, fine
Achchhaa	Well
Achchhaa lagnaa	To like
Aur	And
Baadshaah	King, emperor
Baaees	Twenty two
Baahar	Outside, out
Bahut	Much, many
Bahut	Very
Banaanaa	To make, to build, to prepare
Banvaanaa	To get made
BaRaa	Big, great, large, elder
Bataanaa	To tell , to inform, to explain
Begam	Queen
Bhejnaa	To send, to transmit
Bilkul	Absolutely, quite, entirely
Chaahie	Should, is wanted, is needed
Chaahnaa	To need, to want, to like
Chaar	Four
Chalaa jaanaa	To go away, to depart
ChiTTHee	Letter
ChhoR denaa	To quit, to abundant, to release
ChhoRnaa	To leave, to release, to abundant
ChhoTaa	Small. younger, little
Chup	Quiet, silent
Chup karnaa	To keep quiet
Daak TikaT	Postage stamps

Daalnaa	To put in, to pour
Das	Ten
Dekhnaa	To look, to see, to observe
Der	Late, delay
Dhanyavaad	Thank you, thanks
Din	Day
DonoN	Both
Door	Away, distant, far-off, remote
GaaRee	Car, carriage, coach, vehicle
Ghoomna-phirnaato	To wander, to travel
Gulaam	Slave, the jack of playing cards
HaaN	Yes
Haathee	Elephant
Honaa	To be, to exist, to be born
Idhar	Here
Ikkaa	The ace of playing cards
Inkaa	Their, theirs, his, her, hers
Intazaar	Waiting
Jaanaa	To go
Jaananaa	To know
Jaldee	Hurry, hurriedly, quickly
Jamaa	Collected, deposited
Jamaa karnaa	To collect, to deposited
Jee	Used to show respect
Jitnaa	As much as, as many as
Joota	Shoes
Kaa	Of
Kee	Of
Ke	Of
Kaalaa	Black
Kaaleen	Carpet, rug
KahaaN	Where
Kahnaa	To say, to tell
Kaisaa	How, of what condition
Kal	Yesterday, tomorrow
Kam	Short, less, fee, little
Kameez	Shirt

KapRaa	Cloth
Kapre	Cloths, clothes
Karnaa	To do, to complete
Karvaanaa	To get done, to cause to do
Kelaa	Banana
Ke paas	Nearby, belonging to, with
Khaanaa banaanaa	To cook
Khareedaa jaanaa	To be bought
Khelnaa	To play
Khush	Happy, pleased
Kitaab	Book
Kitna	How much, how
Ko	To, in, on, at
Le jaanaa	To take away
Lenaa	To take
Likhnaa	To write
Maamaa(jee)	Mother's brothers
Maamee(jee)	Mother's brother's wife
MaaN	Mother
Maasee(jee)	Mother's sister
Maataa(jee)	Mother
Maheenaa	Mouth
Main	I
Mandir	Temple
Mausaa(jee)	Mother's sister's husband
Mazaa	Fun, enjoyment
Mazaa aanaa	To have fun, to enjoy
MeN	In, into, among, during
Mera	My, mine
Naanaa(jee)	Maternal grand father
Naanee(jee)	Maternal grand mother
Naatee	Daughter's son
Naatin	Daughter's daughter
Namaste	Expression of greetings
Nanad	Husband's sister
Nandoee	Husband's sister husband
PaRhnaa	To read, to study

Pati	Husband
Patnee	Wife
Pichhlaa	Last, previous
Pitaa(jee)	Father
Potaa	Son's son
Potee	Son's daughter
Rahnaa	To reside, to stay, to remain
Ronaa	To cry
Saalaa	Wife's brother
Saalee	Wife's sister
Saaraa	Entire, whole
SaaRhoo	Wife's sister's husband
Saas	Mother-in-law
Sab	All, entire
Sasur	Father-in-law
Se	From, with, by, since
Shaadee	Marriage, wedding
Sukhee	Happy, contended,
Taaee(jee)	Father's elder brother's wife
Taaoo(jee)	Father's elder brother
THeek	Fine, well, correct, alright
Too	You
Tum	You
Tumhaaraa	Yours, your
Uskaa	His, her, hers
Vaapaas	Back
Vaapaas aanaa	To come back, to return
Ve	They, he, she, those
Vo	He, she, that
Yaad	Memory
Yaad hoona	To remember
YahaaN	Here
Yeh	He, she, this
Ye	They, these

LaVergne, TN USA
08 June 2010
185426LV00001B/12/A

9 780973 948912